SELECT COMMITTEE TO INVESTIGATE THE
JANUARY 6TH
ATTACK ON THE
UNITED STATES CAPITOL

Eighth Select Committee Hearing
July 21, 2022

COMPLETE TRANSCRIPT

# # #

Liz Cheney: "The committee will be in order."

Bennie Thompson: "Good evening. Earlier this week, I received a positive COVID diagnosis. Per CDC guidelines, I've received the initial two shots and all of the boosters. Thus far, I have been blessed to experience very minimal symptoms. Because I'm still quarantined, I cannot participate in person with my colleagues. I've asked our vice chair, Ms. Cheney, to preside over this evening's hearing, including maintaining order in the room and swearing in our witnesses.

"Over the last month and a half, the Select Committee has told the story of a president who did everything in his power to overturn an election. He lied. He bullied. He betrayed his oath. He tried to destroy our democratic institutions. He summoned a mob to Washington. Afterward, on January 6th when he knew that the assembled mob was heavily armed and angry, he commanded the mob to go to the Capitol, and he emphatically commanded the heavily armed mob to fight like hell.

"For the weeks between the November election and January 6th, Donald Trump was a force to be reckoned with. He shrugged off the factuality and legality correct sober advice of his knowledgeable and sensible advisers. Instead, he recklessly blazed a path of lawlessness and corruption, the cost of which democracy be damned.

"And then he stopped. For 187 minutes on January 6th, this man of unbridled destructive energy could not be moved, not by his aides, not by his allies, not by the violent chants of rioters, or the desperate pleas of those facing down the riot. And more tellingly, Donald Trump ignored and disregarded the desperate pleas of his own family, including Ivanka and Don Junior.

"Even though he was the only person in the world who could call off the mob he sent to the Capitol, he could not be moved to rise from his dining room table and walk the few steps down the White House hallway into the press briefing room, where cameras were anxiously and desperately waiting to carry his message to the armed and violent mob savagely beating and killing law enforcement officers ravaging the Capitol and hunting down the vice president and various members of Congress.

"He could not be moved. This evening, my colleagues, Mr. Kinzinger of Illinois and Ms. Luria of Virginia, will take you inside the White House during those 187 minutes. We also remind you of what was happening at the Capitol minute by minute, as the final violent, tragic part of Donald Trump's scheme to cling to power unraveled while he ignored his advisers, stood by, and watched it unfold on television.

"Let me offer a final thought about the Select Committee's work so far. As we've made clear throughout these hearings, our investigation goes forward. We continue to receive new information every day. We continue to hear from witnesses. We will reconvene in September to continue laying out our findings to the American people.

"But as that work goes forward, a number of facts are clear. There can be no doubt that there was a coordinated, multistep effort to overturn an election overseen and directed by Donald Trump. There can be no doubt that he commanded a mob, a mob he knew was heavily armed, violent, and angry, to march on the Capitol to try to stop the peaceful transfer of power.

"And he made targets out of his own vice president and the lawmakers gathered to do the people's work. These facts have gone undisputed, and so there needs to be accountability, accountability under the law, accountability to the American people, accountability at every level, from the local precincts in many states where Donald Trump and his allies attacked election workers for just doing their jobs, all the Way up to the Oval Office, where Donald Trump embraced the legal advice of insurrectionists that a federal judge has already said was a coup in search of a legal theory.

"Our democracy withstood the attack on January 6th. If there is no accountability for January 6th, for every part of this scheme, I fear that we will not overcome the ongoing threat to our democracy. There must be stiff consequences for those responsible. Now I'll turn things over to our vice chair to start telling this story."

Liz Cheney: "Thank you, Mr. Chairman. Without objection, the presiding officer is authorized to declare the committee in recess at any point. Pursuant to House Deposition Authority Regulation 10, I announce that the committee has approved the release of the deposition material presented during today's hearing. And let me begin tonight by wishing Chairman Thompson a rapid recovery from COVID. He has expertly led us through eight hearings so far, and he has brought us to the point we are today.

"In our initial hearing, the chairman and I described what ultimately became Donald Trump's seven part plan to overturn the 2020 presidential election, a plan stretching from before Election Day through January 6th. At the close of today's hearing, our ninth, we will have addressed each element of that plan.

"But in the course of these hearings, we have received new evidence, and new witnesses have bravely stepped forward. Efforts to litigate and overcome immunity and executive privilege claims have been successful, and those continue. Doors have opened, new subpoenas have been issued, and the dam has begun to break.

"And now, even as we conduct our ninth hearing, we have considerably more to do. We have far more evidence to share with the American people and more to gather, so our committee will spend August pursuing emerging information on multiple fronts before convening further hearings this September. Today we know far more about the president's plans and actions to overturn the election than almost all members of Congress did when President Trump was impeached on January 13th, 2021 or when he was tried by the Senate in February of that year.

"Fifty-seven of 100 Senators voted to convict President Trump at that time, and more than 20 others said they were voting against conviction because the president's term had already expired. At the time, the Republican leader of the United States Senate said this about Donald Trump."

[multimedia]

Mitch McConnell: "A mob was assaulting the Capitol in his name. These criminals were carrying his banners, hanging his flags, and screaming their loyalty to him. It was obvious that only President Trump could end this. He was the only one."

Liz Cheney: "Leader McConnell reached those conclusions based on what he knew then without any of the much more detailed evidence you will see today. Lawlessness and violence began at the Capitol on January 6th, 2021 before 1:00 PM and continued until well after darkness fell. What exactly was our commander in chief doing during the hours of violence?

"Today we address precisely that issue. Everything you've heard in these hearings thus far will help you understand President Trump's motives during the violence. You already know Donald Trump's goal: to halt or delay Congress's official proceedings to count certified electoral votes. You know that Donald Trump tried to pressure his vice president to illegally reject votes and delay the proceedings.

"You know he tried to convince state officials and state legislators to flip their electoral votes from Biden to Trump. And you know Donald Trump tried to corrupt our Department of Justice to aid his scheme. But by January 6th, none of that had worked. Only one thing was succeeding on the afternoon of January 6th. Only one thing was achieving President Trump's goal.

"The angry, armed mob President Trump sent to the Capitol broke through security, invaded the Capitol, and forced the vote counting to stop. That mob was violent and destructive, and many came armed. As you will hear, Secret Service agents protecting the vice president were exceptionally concerned about his safety and their own.

"Republican leader Kevin McCarthy was scared, as were others in Congress, even those who themselves helped to provoke the violence. And as you will see today, Donald Trump's own White House counsel, his own White House staff, members of his own family all implored him to immediately intervene to condemn the violence and instruct his supporters to stand down, leave the Capitol, and disperse.

"For multiple hours, he would not. Donald Trump would not get on the phone and order the military or law enforcement agencies to help. And for hours, Donald

Trump chose not to answer the pleas from Congress, from his own party, and from all across our nation to do what his oath required. He refused to defend our nation and our Constitution.

"He refused to do what every American President must. In the days after January 6th, almost no one of any political party would defend President Trump's conduct and no one should do so today. Thank you, and I now recognize the gentlewoman from Virginia."

Elaine Luria: "Thank you, Madam Vice Chair. Article Two of our Constitution requires that the president swear a very specific oath every four years. Every president swears or affirms to faithfully execute the office of President of the United States and to the best of their ability preserve, protect, and defend the Constitution of the United States.

"The president also assumes the constitutional duty to take care that our nation's laws be faithfully executed and is the commander in chief of our military. Our hearings have shown the many ways in which President Trump tried to stop the peaceful transfer of power in the days leading up to January 6th. With each step of his plan he betrayed his oath of office and was derelict in his duty.

"Tonight, we will further examine President Trump's actions on the day of the attack on the Capitol. Early that afternoon, President Trump instructed tens of thousands of supporters at and near the ellipse rally, a number of whom he knew were armed with various types of weapons, to march to the Capitol. After telling the crowd to March multiple times, he promised he would be with them and finished his remarks at 1:10 p.m. like this."

[multimedia]
Donald Trump: **"We're going to walk down and I'll be there with you. We're going to walk down. [Applause] We're going to walk down**

> **anyone you want, but I think right here. We're going to walk down to the Capitol. [Applause] So let's walk down Pennsylvania Avenue."**

Elaine Luria: "By this time, the Vice President was in the Capitol. The joint session of Congress to certify Joe Biden's victory was underway and the Proud Boys and other rioters had stormed through the first barriers and begun the attack.

"Radio communications from law enforcement informed Secret Service and those in the White House Situation Room of these developments in real time. At the direction of President Trump, thousands more rioters marched from the ellipse to the Capitol and they joined the attack. As you will see in great detail tonight, President Trump was being advised by nearly everyone to immediately instruct his supporters to leave the capital disperse and halt the violence.

"Virtually everyone told President Trump to condemn the violence in clear and unmistakable terms. And those on Capitol Hill and across the nation begged President Trump to help. But the former President chose not to do what all of those people begged. He refused to tell the mob to leave until 4:17, when he tweeted out a video statement filmed in the Rose Garden ending with this."

> **[multimedia]**
> **Donald Trump: "So go home. We love you. You're very special. You've seen what happens. You see the way others are treated that are so bad and so evil. I know how you feel. But go home and go home in peace."**

Elaine Luria: "By that time, two pipe bombs had been found at locations near the Capitol including where the Vice President elect was conducting a meeting. Hours of hand-to-hand combat had seriously injured scores of law enforcement officers. The Capitol had been invaded, the electoral count had been halted as members were evacuated.

"Rioters took the floor of the Senate. They rifled through desks and broke into offices, and they nearly caught up to Vice President Pence. Guns were drawn on the House floor and a rioter was shot attempting to infiltrate the chamber. We know that a number of rioters intended acts of physical violence against specific elected officials.

"We know virtually all the rioters were motivated by President Trump's rhetoric that the election had been stolen, and they felt they needed to take their country back. This hearing is principally about what happened inside of the White House that afternoon. From the time when President Trump ended his speech until the moment when he finally told the mob to go home, a span of 187 minutes, more than three hours.

"What you will learn is that President Trump sat in his dining room and watched the attack on television, while his senior most staff, closest advisors, and family members begged him to do what is expected of any American President. I served proudly for 20 years as an officer in the United States Navy. Veterans of our armed forces know firsthand the leadership that's required in a time of crisis, urgent and decisive action that puts duty and country first.

"But on January 6th, when lives and our democracy hung in the balance, President Trump refused to act because of his selfish desire to stay in power. And I yield to the gentleman from Illinois, Mr. Kinzinger."

Adam Kinzinger: "Thank you. Thank you, Ms. Luria. One week after the attack, Republican leader Kevin McCarthy acknowledged the simple truth. President Trump should have acted immediately to stop the violence. During our investigation General Mark Milley, the

Chairman of the Joint Chiefs of Staff, also remarked on the President's failure to act. Let's hear what they had to say."

[multimedia]

Kevin McCarthy: "The President bears responsibility for Wednesday's attack on Congress by mob rioters. He should have immediately denounced the mob when he saw what was unfolding. These facts require immediate action by President Trump."

Mark Milley: "Yeah. You know, Commander in Chief, you got an assault going on on the Capitol of the United States of America. And there's nothing? No call? Nothing? Zero?"

Adam Kinzinger: "Like my colleague from Virginia, I'm a veteran. I served in the Air Force and I serve currently in the Air National Guard. I can tell you that General Milley's reaction to President Trump's conduct is 100 percent correct and so was Leader McCarthy's. What explains President Trump's behavior? Why did he not take immediate action in a time of crisis?

"Because President Trump's plan for January 6th was to halt or delay Congress's official proceeding to count the votes. The mob attacked the Capitol quick — the — the mob attacking the Capitol quickly caused the evacuation of both the House and the Senate. The count ground to an absolute halt and was ultimately delayed for hours.

"The mob was accomplishing President Trump's purpose, so of course he didn't intervene. Here's what'll be clear by the end of this hearing. President Trump did not fail to act during the 187 minutes between leaving the ellipse and telling the mob to go home. He chose not to act. But there were hundreds that day who honored their oaths and put their lives on the line to protect the people inside the Capitol and to safeguard our democracy.

"Many of them are here tonight with us and many more are watching from home. As you already know and we'll see again tonight, their service and sacrifice shines a bright light on President Trump's dishonor and dereliction of duty. I yield to the Vice Chair."

Liz Cheney: "Thank you very much, Mr. Kinzinger. I'd like to begin by welcoming our witnesses this evening. Tonight, we're joined by Mr. Matthew Pottinger. Mr. Pottinger is a decorated former Marine intelligence officer who served this nation on tours of duty in Afghanistan and Iraq. He served in the Trump White House from the first day of the Administration through the early morning hours of January 7th, 2021. The last role in which he served in the White House was as Deputy National Security Advisor to the President of the United States.

"We're also joined by Sarah Matthews. Ms. Matthews started her career in communications, working on Capitol Hill serving on the Republican staffs of several House committees. She then worked as Deputy Press Secretary for President Trump's reelection campaign before joining the Trump White House in June of 2020. She served there as Deputy Press Secretary and Special Assistant to the President until the evening of January 6th, 2021. I will now swear in our witnesses.

"The witnesses will please stand and raise their right hands. Do you swear or affirm under penalty of perjury that the testimony you are about to give is the truth, the whole truth, and nothing but the truth so help you God? Thank you. You may be seated. And let the record reflect that the witnesses answered in the affirmative.

"Thank you both again for being here tonight. Mr. Pottinger, thank you for your service to the nation as well as — as for joining us this evening. Can you please briefly explain what your responsibilities were as Deputy National Security Advisor to the President?"

Matthew Pottinger: "Thank you, Madam, Vice Chair When I started at the White House, I was a Senior Director for Asia on the National Security Council staff. So that was a job that involved helping coordinate the President's Asia policy. I supported the President when he met or interacted with Asian leaders. Later, 2019 I was promoted to the job of Deputy National Security Advisor.

"In that role, I was the Chairman of the deputies committee. That's an NSC meeting of all the deputy cabinet secretaries. We would settle important matters of — of national policy related to — to our national security. And we would also tee up options for the President and for his cabinet members. It was — I — I felt then as I do now that it was a privilege to serve in the White House.

"I'm also very proud of President Trump's foreign policy accomplishments. We were able to finally compete with China. We were also able to broker peace agreements between Israel and — and three Arab states. I mean, those are some examples of the types of policies that I think made our country safer."

Liz Cheney: "Thank you, Mr. Pottinger. And were you in the White House during the attack on the Capitol on January 6th?"

Matthew Pottinger: "For most of the day I was in the White House, although when the — the President was speaking at the rally I was actually offsite at a scheduled meeting with India's ambassador to the United States. The National Security Council staff was not involved in organizing the security for what was a domestic event, the rally.

"But I did return to the White House at roughly 2:30 p.m."

Liz Cheney: "Thank you. And I know my colleagues will have additional questions for you about that afternoon. Let me turn now to you, Ms. Mathews. How did you come to join President Trump's White House staff?"

Sarah Matthews: "Thank you, Madam Vice Chair. As you outlined, I am a lifelong Republican and I joined the Trump reelection campaign in June of 2019. I was one of the first communications staffers actually on board for his reelection campaign. And during that time I traveled all around the country and met Kayleigh McEnany, who was also working on his reelection campaign.

"I worked there for a year and I formed a close relationship with Ms. McEnany and she moved over to the White House in April of 2020 to start as White House Press Secretary and she brought over a group of campaign staff with her. And so I joined her over at the White House in June of 2020 to start as her Deputy."

Liz Cheney: "And were you, Ms. Matthews, at work in the White House on January 6th?"

Sarah Matthews: "Yes, I was working out of the West Wing that day."

Liz Cheney: "Thank you. And now I'd like to recognize the gentlewoman from Virginia and the gentleman from Illinois."

Elaine Luria: "Thank you, Madam Vice Chair. As you've seen in our prior hearings, President Trump summoned the mob to DC on January 6th. Before he went on stage he knew some of them were armed and prepared for combat. During his speech he implored them to march to the Capitol as he had always planned to do. By the time he walked off the stage, his supporters had already breached the outer perimeter of the Capitol at the foot of Capitol Hill.

"Since our last hearings, we've received new testimony from a security professional working in the White House complex on January 6th with access to relevant information and responsibility to report to national security officials. This security official told us that the White House was aware of multiple reports of weapons in the crowd that morning.

"We as a committee are cognizant of the fear of retribution expressed by certain national security witnesses who have come forward to tell the truth. We've therefore taken steps to protect this national security individual's identity.

"Listen to this clip from their testimony."

[multimedia]

Unknown: "What was the consistent message from the people about this idea of the President to walk to the Capitol? To be completely honest, we were all in a state of shock. Because why? Because — because it just — one, I think the actual physical feasibility of doing it. And then also we all knew what that implicated and what that meant.

"That this was no longer a rally, that this was going to move to something else if he physically walked to the Capitol. I — I don't know if you want to use the word insurrection, coup, whatever. We all knew that this would move from a normal, democratic, you know, public event into something else. What was — what was driving that sentiment considering this — this — this part of it, the actual breach of the Capitol hadn't happened yet.

"Why were we alarmed? Right. The President wanted to lead tens of thousands of people to the Capitol. I think that was enough grounds for us to be alarmed."

Elaine Luria: "Even though he understood many of his supporters were armed, the President was still adamant to go to the Capitol when he got off the stage at the ellipse. But his Secret Service detail was equally determined to not let him go. That led to a heated argument with the detail that delayed the departure of the motorcade to the White House.

"We have evidence from multiple sources regarding an angry exchange in the Presidential SUV, including testimony we will disclose today from two witnesses who confirmed that a confrontation occurred. The first witness is a former White House employee with national security responsibilities. After seeing the initial violence at the Capitol on TV, the individual went to see Tony Ornato, the Deputy Chief of Staff in his office."

Elaine Luria: "Mr. Ornato was there with Bobby Engel, the President's lead Secret Service agent. This employee told us that Mr. Ornato said the President was quote, "irate", when Mr. Engel refused to drive him to the Capitol. Mr. Engel did not refute what Mr. Ornato said. The second witness is retired Sergeant Mark Robinson of the DC Police Department who was assigned to the President's motorcade that day. He sat in the lead vehicle with the Secret Service agent responsible for the motorcade, also called the TS agent.

"Here's how Sergeant Robinson remembered the exchange."

[multimedia]

Unknown: "Was there any description of what — of what was occurring in the car?"

Mark Robinson: "No, only that on — the only description I received was that the President was upset and was adamant about going to the Capitol and there was a heated discussion about that."

Unknown: "And when you say heated, is that your word or is that the word that was described by the TS agent?"

Mark Robinson: "No — word described by the TS agent, meaning that the President was upset and he was saying there was a heated argument or discussion about going to the Capitol."

Unknown: "About how many times would you say you've been part of that motorcade with President?"

Mark Robinson: "Ha. Ha. Ha. Probably over 100 times."

Unknown: "And in that 100 times, have you ever witnessed another discussion of an argument or heated discussion with the President where the President was contradicting where he was supposed to go or what the Secret Service believed was safe?"

Mark Robinson: "No."

Elaine Luria: "Like other witnesses, Sergeant Robinson also testified that he was aware that individuals in the crowd were armed."

[multimedia]
Mark Robinson: "Yes, I believe he was on special events channel in — I was monitoring the traffic. So I can hear some of the unit pointing out to individuals that there were individuals along Constitution Avenue that were armed that were up in the trees and I can hear the units responding to those individuals. So there's always a concern when there's a [POTUS] in the area."

<u>Elaine Luria</u>: "And like other witnesses, Sergeant Robinson told us that the President still wanted to travel to the Capitol even after returning to the White House."

[multimedia]
> **Unknown:** "So at the end of the speech, what was the plan supposed to be?"

> **Mark Robinson:** "So at the end of the speech, we do know that while inside the limo, the President was still adamant about going to the Capitol. That's been relayed to me by the TS agent. And so we did [depart] the Ellipse and we responded back to the White House. However, we at the motorcade — POTUS motorcade was placed on standby.

> "And so we were told to stand by on the West exac [ph] until they confirmed whether or not the President was going to go to the Capitol. And so I may have waited, I would just estimate maybe 45 to — 45 minutes to an hour waiting for Secret Service to make that decision."

<u>Elaine Luria</u>: "The motorcade waited at the White House for more than 45 minutes before being released. The

committee is also aware that accounts of the angry confrontation in the Presidential SUV have circulated widely among the Secret Service since January 6th. Recent disclosures have also caused the committee to subpoena yet further information from the Secret Service, which we've begun to receive and will continue to assess.

"The committee is also aware that certain Secret Service witnesses have now retained new private counsel. We anticipate further testimony under oath and other new information in the coming weeks. After the Secret Service refused to take President Trump to the Capitol, he returned to the White House. What you see on the screen is a photo of him inside the Oval Office immediately after he returned from the rally still wearing his overcoat.

"A White House employee informed the President as soon as he returned to the Oval about the riot at the Capitol. Let me repeat that. Within 15 minutes of leaving the stage, President Trump knew that the Capitol was besieged and under attack. At 1:25, President Trump went to the private dining room off the Oval Office.

"From 1:25 until 4:00, the President stayed in his dining room. Just to give you a sense of where the dining room is situated in the West Wing, let's take a look at this floor plan. The dining room is connected to the Oval Office by a short hallway. Witnesses told us that on January 6th President Trump sat in his usual spot at the head of the table facing a television hanging on the wall.

"We know from the employee that the TV was tuned to Fox News all afternoon. Here you can see Fox News on the TV showing coverage of the joint session that was airing that day at 1:25. Other witnesses confirm that President Trump was in the dining room with the TV on for more than two and a half hours. There was no official record of what President Trump did while in the dining room.

"On the screen is the Presidential call log from January 6th. As you can see, there's no official record of President Trump receiving or placing a call between 11:06 and 6:54 pm. As to what the President was doing that afternoon, the Presidential Daily Diary is also silent. It contains no information from the period between 1:21 pm. and 4:03 pm.. There are also no photos of President Trump during this critical period between 1:21 in the Oval Office and when he went outside to the Rose Garden after 4:00. The chief White House photographer wanted to take pictures because it was in her words, very important for his archives and for history, but she was told quote, "no photographs". Despite the lack of photos or an official record, we've learned what President Trump was doing while he was watching TV in the dining room.

"But before we get into that, it's important to understand what he never did that day. Let's watch."

[multimedia]
Unknown: "So are you aware of any phone call by the President of the United States to the Secretary of Defense that day?"

Pat Cipollone: "Not that I'm aware of, no."

Unknown: "Are you aware of any phone call by the President of United States to the attorney general of the United States that day?"

Pat Cipollone: "No."

Unknown: "Are you aware of any phone call by the President of the United States to the Secretary of Homeland Security that day?"

Pat Cipollone: "I'm not aware of that, no."

Unknown: "Did you ever hear the Vice President — or excuse me, the President ask for the National Guard?"

Keith Kellogg: "No."

Unknown: "Did you ever hear the President ask for a law enforcement response?"

Keith Kellogg: "No."

Unknown: "So as somebody who works in the national security space and with the National Security Council here, if there were going to be troops present or called up for a rally in Washington DC, for example, is that something that you would have been aware of?"

Keith Kellogg: "Yeah, I would have."

Unknown: "Do you know if you asked anybody to reach out to any of those that we just listed off? National Guard, DOD, FBI, Homeland Security, Secret Service, Mayor Boswer, or the Capitol Police about the situation in the Capitol."

Nicholas Luna: "I am not aware of any of those requests. No, sir."

Elaine Luria: "We have confirmed in numerous interviews with senior law enforcement and military leaders, Vice President Pence's staff and DC government officials, none of them, not one, heard from President Trump that day. He did not call to issue orders. He did not call to offer assistance. This week we received a —

additional testimony from yet another witness about why the President didn't make any efforts to quell the attack.

The former White House employee with national security responsibilities told us about a conversation with senior advisor, Eric Herschmann, and Pat Cipollone, the top White House lawyer. This conversation was about a pending call from the Pentagon seeking to coordinate on the response to the attack. Mr. Herschmann turned to Mr. Cipollone and said, the President didn't want to do anything.

"And so Mr. Cipollone had to take the call himself. So if President Trump wasn't calling law enforcement or military leaders, what did President Trump spend his time doing that afternoon while he first settled into the dining room? He was calling Senators to encourage them to delay or object to the certification.

"Here's Kayleigh McEnany, his press secretary, to explain."

> **[multimedia]**
> **Unknown: "All right. That says back there and he wants list of Senators. And then he's calling them one by one. Do you know which ones he called?"**
>
> **Kayleigh McEnany: "To the best of my recollection, no. As I say in my notes, he wanted a list of the Senators. And, you know, I left him at that point."**

Elaine Luria: "Because the Presidential call log is empty, we do not yet know precisely which Senators President Trump was calling. But we do know from Rudy Giuliani's phone records that President Trump also called him at 1:39 after he had been told that the riot was underway at the

Capitol. Mr. Giuliani was President Trump's lead election attorney.

"According to the phone records, the President's call with him lasted approximately four minutes. Recall that Fox News was on in the dining room. Let's take a look at what was airing as this call was ending."

> [multimedia]
> **Unknown: "The President, as we all saw, fired this crowd up. They've all — tens of thousands, maybe 100,000 or more have gone down to the Capitol or elsewhere in the city and they're very upset. Now I jumped down as soon as we heard the news that Bret gave you about, Mike Pence. I started talking to these people.**
>
> **"I said, what do you think? One woman, an Air Force veteran from Missouri said she was quote, "disgusted to hear that news and that it was his duty to do something". And I told her, I said there's nothing in the Constitution unilaterally that Vice President Pence could do. She said, that doesn't matter. He should have fought for Trump."**

Elaine Luria: "At 1:49, here's what was happening at the Capitol with President Trump's fired up supporters."

> [multimedia]
> **Unknown: "We're going to give — fire a warning. We're going to try to get compliance, but this is now effectively a riot. 1:49 hours declaring it a riot."**

Elaine Luria: "What did President Trump do at 1:49 as the DC police at the same time were declaring a riot at the Capitol. As you can see on the screen, he tweeted out a link to the recording of his Ellipse speech. This was the same speech in which he knowingly sent an armed mob to the Capitol, but President Trump made no comment about the lawlessness and the violence.

"I yield to the gentleman from Illinois."

Adam Kinzinger: "The next action President Trump took was to tweet at 2:24 pm What happened during the 35 minutes between his last tweet at 1:49 and 2:24? His staff repeatedly came into the room to see him and plead that he make a strong public statement condemning the violence and instructing the mob to leave the Capitol.

"He did not relent until after 4:00 when he went out to go to the Rose Garden to film his now infamous go home message. Pat Cipollone was a top White House lawyer. Here's what he told us about his reaction to seeing the violence and his advice throughout the afternoon."

> **[multimedia]**
> **Unknown: "When did you first realize that there was actually violence or rioting?"**
>
> **Pat Cipollone: "I first realized it may have been on television or may have been Tony or may have been Philbin. But I found out that people were, you know, they weren't in the Capitol yet, but they were, you know, and I then I started watching it and, you know, then I was aware."**
>
> **Unknown: "What specifically did you think needed to be done?"**
>
> **Pat Cipollone: "I think I was pretty clear. There needed to be an immediate and forceful response statement – public statement that people need to leave the Capitol now."**

Unknown: "My question is exactly that, that it sounds like you from the very outset of violence at the Capitol, right around 2:00, were pushing for a strong statement that people should leave the Capitol. Is that right?"

Pat Cipollone: "I was, and others were as well."

Unknown: "Pat, you said that you expressed your opinion forcefully. Could you tell us exactly how you did that?"

Pat Cipollone: "Yeah, I can't — I don't have, you know, I have to — on the privilege issue, I can't talk about conversations with the President, but I can generically say that I said, you know, people need to be told, there needs to be a public announcement fast that they need to leave the Capitol."

Unknown: "And Pat, could you let us know approximately when you said that?"

Pat Cipollone: "Approximately when? Almost immediately after I found out people were getting into the Capitol or approaching the Capitol in a way that was — was violent."

Unknown: "Do you remember any discussion with Mark Meadows with respect to his view that the President didn't want to do anything? Was somehow of resistant to wanting to say something [inaudible] suggest."

Pat Cipollone: "Tony [inaudible] just to be clear, many people suggested it. Yeah, not just me. Many people felt the same way. I'm sure I had conversations with Mark about this during the course of the day and expressed my opinion very forcefully that this needs to be done."

Unknown: "So your advice was to tell people to leave the Capitol and it took over two hours when there were subsequent statements made, tweets put forth, that in your view were insufficient. Did you continue, Mr. Cipollone, throughout the period of time up until 4:17 — continue, you and others, to push for a stronger statement?"

Pat Cipollone: "Yes."

Unknown: "Were you joined in that effort by Ivanka Trump?"

Pat Cipollone: Yes.

Unknown: "Eric Herschmann?"

Pat Cipollone: "Yes."

Unknown: "And Mark Meadows?"

Pat Cipollone: "Yes."

Cassidy Hutchinson: "White House counsel's office wanted there to be a strong statement out to condemn the rioters. I'm confident in that. I'm confident that Ivanka Trump wanted there to be a strong statement to condemn the rioters. I don't know the private conversation she had with Mr. Trump. But I remember when she came to the office one time with White House counsel's office — when she came to the chief of staff's office with White House counsel's office, she was talking about the speech later that day and trying to get her dad on board with saying something that was more direct than he had wanted to at the time and throughout the afternoon."

Pat Cipollone: "I think Mark also wanted — got — I remember him getting Ivanka involved, because — said get Ivanka down here because he thought that would be important. I don't think Jared was there in the morning, but I think he came later. I remember thinking it was important to get him in there too. And — and of course, Pat Philbin, you know, was expressing the same things.

"I mean, Pat Philbin, you know, was very — as I said, I don't think there was one of these meetings where — there might have been, but for the most part, I remember the both of us going down together, going back, getting on phone calls. He was also very clearly expressing this view."

Adam Kinzinger: "Pat Cipollone and Cassidy Hutchinson, an aide to Chief of Staff Mark Meadows, also told us about the hang Mike Pence chants. As you will see, Mr. Cipollone recalled conversations about those chants in the West Wing, but he relied on executive privilege to maintain confidentiality over his and others' direct communications with the President.

"Although Mr. Cipollone was unwilling to provide more detail, Ms. Hutchinson provided more explicit information, filling in those blanks. See that for yourself."

[multimedia]
Cassidy Hutchinson: "It wasn't until Mark hung up the phone, handed it back to me. I

went back to my desk. A couple of minutes later, him and Pat came back, possibly Eric Herschmann too. I'm pretty sure Eric Herschmann was there, but I'm — I'm confident it was Pat that was there. I remember Pat saying something to the effect of, Mark, we need to do something more.

"They're literally calling for the vice president to be effing hung. And Mark had responded something to the effect of, you heard him, Pat. He thinks Mike deserves it. He doesn't think they're doing anything wrong. To which Pat said something, this is effing crazy, we need to be doing something more, briefly stepped into Mark's office."

Unknown: "Do you remember any discussion at any point during the day about rioters at the Capitol chanting hang Mike Pence?"

Pat Cipollone: "Yes, I remember — I remember hearing that about that, yes. I don't know if I observed that myself on TV."

Unknown: "I'm just curious. I understand the — the privilege line you've drawn, but do you remember what you can share with us about the discussion about those chants, the hang Mike Pence chants?"

Pat Cipollone: "I can tell you my view of that."

Unknown: "Yeah, please."

Pat Cipollone: "My view of that is that is outrageous. And for anyone to suggest such a thing of the vice president of the United States, for people in that crowd to be chanting that I thought was terrible. I thought it was outrageous and wrong, and I expressed that very clearly."

Adam Schiff: "With respect to your conversations with Mr. Meadows, though, did you specifically raise your concern over the vice president with him, and — and how did he respond?"

Pat Cipollone: "I believe I raised the concern about the vice president, and I — and I — again, the nature of his response, without recalling exactly was he — you know, people were doing all that they could."

Adam Schiff: "And — and what about the president? Did he indicate whether he thought the president was doing what needed to be done to protect the vice president?"

Unknown: "Privilege. You have to assert it. That question would –"

Pat Cipollone: "That would call for — I'm being instructed on privilege."

Unknown: "I see."

Adam Kinzinger: "In addition, Mr. Cipollone testified that it would have been feasible, as commentators on television were suggesting, for President Trump to immediately appear at the podium in the press room to address the nation."

[multimedia]
Unknown: "Would it have been possible at any moment for the president to walk down to the podium in the briefing room and tell — talk to

the nation at anytime between when you first gave him that advice at 2:00 and 4:17 when the video statement went? Would that have been possible?"

Pat Cipollone: "Would it have been possible?"

Unknown: "Yes."

Pat Cipollone: "Well, yes, it would have been possible."

Adam Kinzinger: "We just heard Mr. Cipollone say that President Trump could have gone to the press briefing room to issue a statement at any moment. To give you a sense of just how easy that would have been, let's take a look at a map of the West Wing. As we saw earlier, the president's private dining room is at the bottom of the map.

"The press briefing room is at the top highlighted in blue, and the Rose Garden, where the President ultimately filmed his go home video, is on the right next to the Oval Office, and that's highlighted in green. Ms. Matthews, how quickly could the president have gotten on camera in the press briefing room to deliver a statement to the nation?"

Sarah Matthews: "So, as you outlined, it would take probably less than 60 seconds from the Oval Office dining room over to the press briefing room. And for folks that might not know, the briefing room is the room that you see the White House press secretary do briefings from with the podium and the blue backdrop. And there's a camera that is on in there at all times.

"And so, if the president had wanted to make a statement and address the American people, he could have been on camera almost instantly. And conversely, the White House press corps has offices that are located directly behind the briefing room. And so, if he had wanted to make an address from the Oval Office, we could have assembled the White House press corps probably in a matter of minutes to get them into the Oval for him to do an on camera address."

Adam Kinzinger: "Thank you. Other witnesses have given us their views on that question. For example, General Keith Kellogg told us that some staff were concerned that a live appearance by the president at the microphones at that moment could actually make matters worse. He told us he recommended against doing a press conference because, during his four years in the Trump administration, "There wasn't a single clean press conference we had had." President Trump's advisers knew his state of mind at that moment, and they were worried about what he would say in unscripted comments.

"I yield to the gentlewoman from Virginia."

Elaine Luria: "Thank you. As you've heard, by 2:00 multiple staff members in the White House recognized that a serious situation was underway at the Capitol. Personally, I recall being evacuated from the House office building where we're sitting by — before this time. It was due to the discovery of two pipe bombs in nearby buildings.

"Ms. Mathews, around the same time, you were watching the violence unfold on television and social media with colleagues, including with Ben Williamson, a senior aide to Mark Meadows and the acting director of communications. You told us that before President Trump's sent his next tweet at 2:24, Mr. Williamson got up to go see Mr. Meadows and you got up to go see Kayleigh McEnany.

"Why did you both do that?"

Sarah Matthews: "So, Ben and I were watching the coverage unfold from one of the offices in the West Wing. And we both recognized that the situation was escalating and it was escalating quickly, and that the president needed to be out there immediately to tell these people to go home and condemn the violence that we were seeing.

"So, I told him that I was going to make that recommendation to Kayleigh, and he said he was going to make the same recommendation to the chief of staff, Mark Meadows."

Elaine Luria: "Thank you. And one of your colleagues in the press office, Judd Deere, told us he also went to see Ms. McEnany at that time. Let's hear what he said about this critical period of time right as the rioters were getting into the Capitol."

> [multimedia]
> **Unknown: "And why did you think it was necessary to say something?"**
>
> **Judd Deere: "Well, I mean, it appears that individuals are storming the US Capitol building. They also appear to be supporters of Donald Trump, who may have been in attendance at the rally. We're going to need to say something."**
>
> **Unknown: "And did you have a view as to what should be said about the White House?"**
>
> **Judd Deere: "If I recall, I told Kayleigh that I thought that we needed to encourage individuals to stop, to respect law enforcement, and to go home."**

Elaine Luria: "Although President Trump was aware of the ongoing riot, he did not take any immediate action to address the lawlessness. Instead, at 2:03, he called Rudy Giuliani again, and that call lasted for over eight minutes. Moments later at 2:13, rioters broke into the Capitol itself. One of the Proud Boys charged with seditious conspiracy, Dominic Pezzola, used an officer's shield to smash a window, and rioters flooded into the building."

> [multimedia]
> **Unknown: "[Crowd noise] Go, go, go, go. Go in the Capitol. Go, go, go."**

Elaine Luria: "As rioters were entering the building, the Secret Service held Vice President Pence in his office right off the Senate chamber for 13 minutes as they worked to clear a safe path to a secure location. Now listen to some of that radio traffic and see what they were seeing as the protesters got just feet away from where the Vice President was holding."

> [multimedia]
> **Unknown: "They're taking the building. Hold. Harden that door up. If you are moving, we need to move now. Copy. If we lose any more time, we may have — we may lose the ability to — to leave. So, if we're going to leave, we need to do it now. They've gained access to the second floor and I've got public about five feet from me down here below.**
>
> **"Ok, copy. They are on the second floor moving in now. We may want to consider getting out and leaving now, copy? Will we encounter the people once we make our way? Repeat? Encounter any individuals if we made our way to the — to the — There's six officers between us and the people that are five to 10 feet away from me. Stand by. I'm going to down to evaluate.**

"Go ahead. We have a clear shot if we move quickly. We've got smoke downstairs. Stand by, unknown smoke from downstairs. By the protesters? Is that route compromised? We have the — is secure. However, we will bypass some protesters that are being contained. There is smoke, unknown what kind of smoke it is, copy?

"Clear. We're coming out now, all right? Make a way."

Elaine Luria: "The president's National Security Council staff was listening to these developments and tracking them in real time. On the screen, you can see excerpts from the chat logs among the national — among the president's National Council — National Security Council staff. At 2:13, the staff learned that the rioters were kicking in the windows at the Capitol.

"Three minutes later, the staff said the vice president was being pulled, which meant agents evacuated him from the Senate floor. At 2:24, the staff noted that the Secret Service agents at the Capitol did not "sound good right now." Earlier you heard from a security professional who had been working in the White House complex on January 6th with access to relevant information and a responsibility to report to national security officials.

"We asked this person what was meant by the comment that the Secret Service agents did not "sound good right now." In the following clip of that testimony, which has been modified to protect the individual's identity, the professional discusses what they heard from listening to the incoming radio traffic that day."

[multimedia]
Unknown: "Ok. That last entry in the page is service at the capital does not sound good right

now. Correct. What does that mean? Well, members of the VP detail at this time were starting to fear for their own lives. There were a lot of — there was a lot of yelling, a lot of — a lot of very personal calls over the radio, so it was disturbing.

"I don't like talking about it. But there — there were calls to say goodbye to family members, so on and so forth. It was getting — for — for whatever the reason was on the ground, the VP detail thought that this was about to get very ugly. And do — did you hear that over the radio? Correct. Ok. What was the response by the agents who were — Secret Service agents who were there?"

<u>Unknown</u>: "Everybody kept saying — you know, at that point it was just reassurances or — I think there were discussions of reinforcements coming. But — but again, it was just chaos, and they were just obviously, you've conveyed that's disturbing. But what — what prompted you to put it into an entry as it states there, Service at the Capitol? They were running out of options and they were getting nervous. It — it sounds like we're — that we came very close to either service having to use lethal options or — or worse.

"Like, at — at that point I don't know. Is the VP compromised? Is the detail comp — like, I — I don't know. Like, we didn't have visibility, but it doesn't — if they're screaming and — and saying things like say goodbye to the family, like, the floor needs to know this is going to on a whole nother[Ph] level soon."

Elaine Luria: "As this next video shows, the rioters' anger was foc — focused primarily on Vice President Mike Pence."

[multimedia]

Janet Buhler: "This woman cames up to the side of us and she says Pence folded. So it was kind of, like, Ok, well — in my mind I was thinking, well that's it. You know. Well, my son-in-law looks at me and he says I want to go in."

Unknown: "What percentage of the crowd is going to the Capitol?"

Jessica Watkins: "100 percent. It is — it has spread like wildfire that Pence has betrayed us. And everybody is marching on the Capitol, all million of us. It's insane."

Unknown: "Mike Pence will not stick up for Donald Trump. Mike Pence, traitor. Mike Pence has screwed us, in case you haven't heard yet. What happened? What happened? I keep hearing that Mike Pence has screwed us. That's the word. I keep hearing reports that Mike Pence has screwed us. Did people appear angry as you were walking to the Capitol?

"Yeah, a lot of people — a lot of people seemed like they were very upset. Tell us some of the things they were saying, if you recall."

Stephen Ayers: "Oh, there was — they were saying all type — you know, people were screaming all types of stuff. They were mad that Vice President Pence was going to accept the electoral laws. I mean, it was — I mean it was a load of — you can — if you can think it up that's — you are hearing it."

Unknown: "I believe that Vice President Pence was going to certify the electoral votes and — or not certify them. But I guess that's just changed. Correct? And it's a very big disappointment. I think there's several hundred thousand people here that are very disappointed."

Elaine Luria: "President Trump did not try to calm his thousands of disappointed supporters. Instead at almost the same moment violence was getting completely out of hand, Donald Trump sent his 2:24 tweet. The President said Mike Pence didn't have the courage to do what should have been done to protect our country and our Constitution.

"Despite knowing the Capitol had been breached and the mob was in the building, President Trump called Mike Pence a coward and placed all the blame on him for not stopping the certification. He put a target on his own Vice President's back. Mr. Pottinger and Miss Mathews, when we asked you about your reaction to seeing the 2:24 tweet in real time, you both use the same imagery to describe it. President Trump was adding fuel to the fire.

"Mr. Pottinger, you made the decision to resign after seeing this tweet. Can you please tell us why?"

Matthew Pottinger: "Yes. So that was the — pretty soon after I'd — or shortly before I'd gotten back to the White House. I'd come from off site. I began to see for the first time those images on TV of the chaos that was unfolding at the Capitol. One of my aides handed me a sheet of paper that contained the tweet that you just read.

"I — I read it and was quite disturbed by it. I — I was disturbed and worried to see that the President was attacking Vice President Pence for doing his constitutional duty. So the tweet looked to me like the opposite of what — what we really needed at that moment, which was a de-escalation. And that's why I had said earlier that it looked like fuel being poured on the fire.

"So that was the moment that I decided that I was going to resign, that that would be my last day at the White House. I — I simply didn't want to be associated with — with the events that were unfolding on the Capitol."

Elaine Luria: "Thank you. And Ms. Matthews, what was your reaction to the President's tweet about Vice President Pence?"

Sarah Matthews: "So, it was obvious that the situation at the Capitol was violent and escalating quickly. And so I thought that the tweet about the Vice President was the last thing that was needed in that moment. And I — I remember thinking that this was going to be bad for him to tweet this because it was essentially him giving the green light to these people, telling them that what they were doing at the steps of the Capitol and entering the Capitol was Ok, that they were justified in their anger.

"And he shouldn't have been doing that. He should have been telling these people to go home and to leave and to condemn the violence that we were seeing. And I'm someone who has worked with him. You know, I worked on the campaign, traveled all around the country going to countless rallies with him. And I've seen the impact that his words have on his supporters.

"He — they truly latch on to every word and every tweet that he says. And so I think that in that moment for him to tweet out the message about Mike Pence, it was him pouring gasoline on the fire and making it much worse."

Elaine Luria: "Thank you both. And let's watch what others also told us about their reactions to this tweet."

[multimedia]
Pat Cipollone: "I don't remember when exactly I heard about that tweet, but my reaction to it is that's a — a terrible tweet. And I disagreed with the sentiment and I thought it was wrong."

Unknown: "What was your reaction when you saw that tweet?"

Judd Deere: "Extremely unhelpful."

Unknown: "Why?"

Judd Deere: "It — it — it wasn't the message that we needed at — at that time. It wasn't going to — the — the scenes at the US Capitol were only getting worse at that point. This was not going to help that."

Unknown: "Were you concerned it could make it worse?"

Judd Deere: "Certainly."

Liz Cheney: "Ms. Hutchinson, what was your reaction when you saw this tweet?"

Cassidy Hutchinson: "As a staffer that works to always represent the Administration to the best of my ability and to showcase the good things that he had done for the country, I remember feeling frustrated, disappointed, and really it — it felt personal. I — I was

really sad. As an American, I was disgusted. It was unpatriotic.

"It was un-American. We were watching the Capitol building get defaced over a lie."

<u>**Elaine Luria**</u>: "As you will see, at 2:26, the Vice President had to be evacuated to safety a second time and came within 40 feet of the rioters. The attack escalated quickly right after the tweet."

[multimedia]
<u>Unknown</u>: [Inaudible]

<u>**Elaine Luria**</u>: "During this chaos, what did President Trump do at that point? He went back to calling Senators to try to further delay the electoral count. While the Vice President was being evacuated from the Senate, President Trump called Senator Tommy Tuberville, one of his strongest supporters in the Senate. As Senator Tuberville later recalled, he had to end the call so that he could evacuate the Senate chamber himself.

"Let's listen."

[multimedia]
<u>**Tommy Tuberville**</u>: **"He called — didn't call my phone. Called somebody else and they handed it to me. And I — I basically told him, I said Mr. President, we're — we're not doing much work here right now because they just took our Vice President out. And matter of fact I'm gonna have to hang up on you. I've got to leave."**

<u>**Elaine Luria**</u>: "Senator Josh Hawley also had to flee. Earlier that afternoon before the joint session started, he walked across the east front of the Capitol. As you can see in this photo, he raised his fist in solidarity with the

protesters already amassing at the security gates. We spoke with a Capitol police officer who was out there at the time.

"She told us that Senator gest — Senator Hawley's gesture riled up the crowd, and it bothered her greatly because he was doing it in a safe space, protected by the officers and the barriers. Later that day Senator Hawley fled after those protesters he helped to rile up stormed the Capitol. See for yourself."

[multimedia]
Unknown: [Inaudible]

"Think about what we've seen, undeniable violence at the Capitol. The Vice President being evacuated to safety by the Secret Service. Senators running through the hallways of the Senate to get away from the mob. As the Commander in Chief, President Trump was oath and duty bound to protect the Capitol.

"His senior staff understood that."

[multimedia]
Liz Cheney: "Do — do you believe, Jared, that the President has an obligation to ensure a peaceful transfer of power?"

Jared Kushner: "Yes."

Liz Cheney: "And do you think the President has an obligation to defend all three branches of our government?"

Jared Kushner: "I believe so."

Liz Cheney: "And I assume you also would agree the President has a particular obligation to take care that the laws be faithfully executed."

Pat Cipollone: "That is one of the President's obligations, correct."

Liz Cheney: "No, I mean, I asked what his duty is."

Keith Kellogg: "Well, I mean, there's a — there's a constitutional duty — I — what he has — he's the Commander in Chief. And that was the — the — that was my biggest issue with him as National Security Advisor."

Elaine Luria: "Rather than uphold his duty to the Constitution, President Trump allowed the mob to achieve the delay that he hoped would keep him in power. I reserve."

Liz Cheney: "The gentlewoman reserves. I request that those in the hearing room remain seated until the Capitol Police have escorted members and witnesses from the room. I now declare the committee in recess for a period of approximately 10 minutes. The committee will be in order. I now recognize the gentleman from Illinois.

"The committee will be in order. I now recognize the gentleman from Illinois."

Adam Kinzinger: "We left at the recess just after President Trump's 2:24 tweet attacking the Vice President. By this time the President had been in his dining room for an hour. I want you to just think of what you would have done if you were in his shoes and had the power to end the violence. You would have immediately and forcefully told the rioters to stop and leave.

"Like, stop and leave. Done. As you heard, that's exactly what his senior staff had been urging him to do, but he resisted and he kept resisting for another almost two hours.

"In the meantime, all the President did was post two tweets, one at 2:38 and the other at 3:13. One said quote, "stay peaceful". The other said quote, "remain peaceful". But the President already knew that the mob was attacking the police and had invaded the Capitol.

"Neither tweet condemned the violence or told the mob to leave the Capitol and disperse. To appreciate how obvious it was that President Trump was not meeting this moment, it's helpful to look at the real time reactions of his own son, Don Jr to the first tweet captured in a series of text messages with Mark Meadows.

"I warn the audience that these messages contain some strong language. As you can see Don Jr's first — Don Jr first texted Mr. Meadows at 2:53. He wrote, he's got to condemn this shit ASAP. The Capitol Police tweet is not enough. Mr. Meadows replied, I am pushing it hard, I agree. Don Jr responded, this is one you go to the mattresses on. They will try to fuck his entire legacy if this — on this if it gets worse.

"Here's what Don Jr. told us he meant by go to the mattresses."

> **[multimedia]**
> **Unknown: "At 2:58 when you say that he need — that Mr. Meadows needs to go to the mattresses on this issue, when you say go to the mattresses, what does that mean?"**
>
> **Donald Trump Jr.: "It's just a reference for going all in. I think it's a Godfather reference."**

Adam Kinzinger: "Sean Hannity agreed, and he also turned to Mark Meadows for help after the President's second tweet. As you can see, Mr. Hannity texted at 3:31 to say, Trump needed to deliver a statement to the nation telling the rioters to leave the Capitol. Mr. Meadows responded, that he was quote, "on it". Don Jr and Sean Hannity were not the only ones who implored Mr. Meadows to get the President to speak to the nation and tell the mob to leave, to go home, go home.

"Throughout the attack, Mr. Meadows received texts from Republican members of Congress, from current and former Trump administration officials, from media personalities, and from friends. Like President Trump's staff, they knew President Trump had to speak publicly to get the mob to stop. Let's look at just a few of these text messages.

"Fox News personality, Laura Ingraham, said the President needs to tell the people in the Capitol to go home. Former chief of staff, Mick Mulvaney, urged Mark, he needs to stop this now. Fox News personality, Brian Kilmeade, said, please get him on TV. Destroying everything that you guys have accomplished.

"When we interviewed White House counsel, Pat Cipollone, he told us that he knew the President's two tweets were not enough. Let's listen to what he said."

> **[multimedia]**
> **Unknown: "I think the question is did you believe the tweets were not anything about your advice to the President?"**
>
> **Pat Cipollone: "No, I believe more needed to be done. I believed that a public statement needed to be made."**
>
> **Liz Cheney: "When you talk about others on the staff thinking more should be done or thinking that the President needed to tell people to go home, who — who would you put in that category?"**

Pat Cipollone: "Well, I — I would put it Pat Philbin, Eric Herschmann, overall Mark Meadows, Ivanka, once Jared got there Jared, General Kellogg. I'm probably missing some, but those are — Kayleigh I think was — was there, but I don't — Dan Scavino."

Liz Cheney: "And who on the staff did not want people to leave the Capitol?"

Pat Cipollone: "On the staff?"

Liz Cheney: "In the White House, how about?"

Pat Cipollone: "I don't — I — I can't think of anybody, you know, on that day who didn't want people to get out of the — the Capitol once the — you know, particularly once the violence started, no. I mean –"

Adam Schiff: "What about the president?"

Liz Cheney: "Yeah."

Pat Cipollone: "She said the staff, so I answered."

Liz Cheney: "No, I said in the White House."

Pat Cipollone: "Oh, I'm sorry. I — I apologize. I thought you said who — who else on the staff. I — I — I can't reveal communications, but obviously I think, you know, — yeah."

Adam Kinzinger: "Let's pause on that last statement. Although Pat Cipollone is being careful about executive privilege, there really is no ambiguity about what he said. Almost everybody wanted President Trump to instruct the mob to disperse. President Trump refused. To understand how inadequate the president's tweets were, let's examine his 2:38 tweet in more detail.

"For context, here's what was happening at that time."

[multimedia]

Unknown: "They broke the glass right there. Everybody stay down. Get down. Lower barricade, there's people flooding the hallways outside. We have no way out. We were just told that there has been teargas in the Rotunda, and we're being instructed to each of us get a gasmask. We went from a peaceful protest, and this is a very dangerous situation right now.

"The — there are — I'm being told these protesters on the inside are around both chambers, and there is now tear gas inside the Capitol Rotunda. In fact, members locked in the House are being instructed to put on masks."

Adam Kinzinger: "Ms. Matthews, after President Trump's tweet about Vice President Pence, you told us you spoke to — immediately you spoke to Kayleigh McEnany. What did you tell her and where did she go afterwards?"

Sarah Matthews: "After the tweet about the vice president, I found Kayleigh and told her that I thought the president needed to immediately send out a tweet that condemned the violence that we were seeing, and that there needed to be a call to action to tell these people to leave the Capitol. And she agreed and walked over to the Oval Dining Room to find the president."

Adam Kinzinger: "We interviewed Ms. McEnany and others who — who were in the dining room with the president, urging him to put out a statement. Ms. Matthews, Ms. McEnany told us she came right back to the press office after meeting with the president about this particular tweet. What did she tell you about what happened in that dining room?"

Sarah Matthews: "When she got back, she told me that a tweet had been sent out. And I told her that I thought the tweet did not go far enough, that I thought there needed to be a call to action and he needed to condemn the violence. And we were in a room full of people, but people weren't paying attention. And so, she looked directly at me and, in a hushed tone, shared with me that the president did not want to include any sort of mention of peace in that tweet, and that it took some convincing on their part, those who were in the room.

"And she said that there was a back and forth, going over different phrases to find something that he was comfortable with. And it wasn't until Ivanka Trump suggested the phrase stay peaceful that he finally agreed to include it."

Adam Kinzinger: "The president resisted writing stay peaceful in a tweet. He told Mark Meadows that the rioters were doing what they should be doing and the rioters understood they were doing what President Trump wanted them to do. President Trump's message was heard clearly by Stop The Steal organizer Ali Alexander. At 2:38, he told another organizer, "POTUS is not ignorant of what his words would do." Rioters storming the Capitol also heard President Trump's message.

"In this video, you'll see surveillance footage from the Rotunda that shows a group of Oath Keepers, including Jessica Watkins, who's been charged with seditious conspiracy. You'll hear her walkie-talkie communications with others as they share intelligence and communicate about President Trump's 2:38 tweet in real time.

"Again, we warn the audience that this clip also contains strong language."

[multimedia]

Unknown: "CNN just said that they evacuated all members of Congress into a safety room. There is no safe place in the United States for any of these motherfuckers right now, let me tell you. I hope they understand that we are not joking around. Military principle 105, Military Principle 105, cave means grave. Trump just tweeted please support our Capitol Police.

"They are on our side. Do not harm them. That's saying a lot by what he didn't say. He didn't say not to do anything to the Congressmen. Well, he did not ask them to stand down. He just said stand by the Capitol Police. They are on our side and they are good people. So, it's getting real down there. I got it on TV, and it's — it's looking pretty friggin radical to me. CNN said that Trump has egged this on, that he is egging it on, and that he is watching the country burn two weeks before he leaves office.

"He is not leaving office. I don't give a shit what they say. And we are in the mezzanine. We are in the main dome right now. We are rocking it. They're throwing grenades. They're frickin shooting people with paintballs, but we're in here. Be safe, be safe. God bless and Godspeed, and keep going. Get it, Jess.

"Do your shit. This is what we fucking lived up for, everything we fucking trained for. Took over the Capitol, overran the Capitol. We're in the fucking Capitol complex."

Adam Kinzinger: "We've now seen how President Trump's supporters reacted to his tweets. Mr. Pottinger, you told us that you consider the tweets sent to this point to be "wholly inadequate given the urgency of the crisis." What in your view would have been needed?"

Matthew Pottinger: "Yeah, I — it was insufficient. And I think what — you could count me among those who was hoping to see an unequivocal strong statement clearing out the Capitol, telling people to stand down, leave, go home. I — I think that's what we were hoping for."

Adam Kinzinger: "So, something a lot more kind of definitive and not ambiguous –"

Matthew Pottinger: "Yes."

John Kirby: "Because he has that power over his folks. Ms. Matthews, you told us about a colleague who said during the attack that the president should not condemn the violence. Can you please tell us about how that — about that moment and your reaction?"

Sarah Matthews: "Yes. So, a conversation started in the press office after the president sent out those two tweets that I deemed were insufficient. And a colleague suggested that the president shouldn't condemn the violence because they thought it would "handing a win" to the media if he were to condemn his supporters. And I disagreed.

"I thought that we should condemn the violence and condemn it unequivocally. And I thought that he needed to include a call to action and to tell these people to go home, and a debate ensued over it. And I became visibly frustrated, and my colleagues were well aware of that. And I couldn't believe that we were arguing over this in the middle of the West Wing, talking about the politics of a tweet, being concerned with handing the media a win when we had just watched all of that violence unfold at the Capitol.

"And so, I motioned up at the TV and I said do you think it looks like we're effing winning? Because I don't think it does. And I again reiterated that I thought that the president needed to condemn the violence because it didn't matter if it was coming from the left or the right, that you should condemn violence 100 percent of the time."

Adam Kinzinger: "We've — we've heard this evening how everyone in the president's orbit was pushing him to do more, to tell the mob to leave the Capitol. One of these people — one of those people was Republican leader Kevin McCarthy. He managed to get the president on the phone and told him to call off his supporters. As you will hear, the president refused, and so Leader McCarthy reached out for help to Ivanka Trump, who was at the White House, and Jared Kushner, who that afternoon had just arrived back on a flight from the Middle East."

> **[multimedia]**
> **Unknown: "So, at some point in the afternoon, Mr. McCarthy placed a phone call to Mr. Scavino's desk line, and it was transferred to the president. Is that correct?"**
>
> **Molly Michael: "That's generally what I recall."**
>
> **Unknown: "Okay. Were you involved in making that — transferring that call?"**
>
> **Molly Michael: "I—I—Yes."**

Unknown: "Okay. Where was the president at the time that he took that call?"

Molly Michael: "He was in the dining room."

Unknown: "Would you personally reach out to the president for more support?"

Mark Meadows: "I've already talked to the president. I called him. I think we need to make a statement, make sure that we can calm individuals down.

Unknown: Did Mr. McCarthy indicate that he had been in touch with President Trump?"

Marc Short: "He indicated that he had had some conversation, I don't recall whether it was with the — with the president or with somebody at the White House. But I think he — he expressed frustration that — not taking the circumstance as seriously as they should in that moment."

Jaime Herrera Beutler: "You know, I asked Kevin McCarthy, who's the Republican leader, about this and — and he said she called Donald — he finally got through to Donald Trump. And he said you have got to get on TV, you've got to get on Twitter, you've got to call these people off. You know what the president said to him? This is as it's happening.

"He said, well, Kevin, these aren't my people. You know, these are — these are Antifa. And Kevin responded and said no, they're your people. They literally just came through my office windows and my staff are running for cover. I mean, they're running for their lives.

You need to call them off. And the president's response to Kevin, to me, was chilling.

"He said, well, Kevin, I guess they're just more upset about the election, you know, theft than you are. And that's — you know, you've seen widespread reports of — of Kevin McCarthy and the president having a — basically a swearing conversation. That's when the swearing commenced, because the president was basically saying, nah, I — I'm okay with this."

Unknown: "Leader McCarthy, the president of the United States has a briefing room steps from the Oval Office. It is — the cameras are hot 24/7, as you know. Why hasn't he walked down and said that now?"

Kevin McCarthy: "I conveyed to the president what I think is best to do, and I'm hopeful the president will do it."

Unknown: "And have you spoken with his chief of staff?"

Kevin McCarthy: "I've spoken to the president. I've spoken to other people in there and to the White House as well."

Unknown: "Who else reached out to Mr. Trump that you know of that afternoon about the attack on the Capitol?"

Julie Radford: "I believe at one point McCarthy did."

Jared Kushner: "So, my — I heard my phone ringing, turn the shower off, saw it was Leader

McCarthy, who I had a good relationship with. He told me it was getting really ugly over at the Capitol and said, please, you know, anything you could do to help, I would appreciate it. I don't recall a specific ask, just anything you could do. Again, I got the sense that, you know, they were — they were — you know, they were scared."

Unknown: "They meaning Mr. — Leader McCarthy and people on the Hill because of the violence?"

Jared Kushner: "That he — he was scared, yes."

Adam Kinzinger: "Think about that. Leader McCarthy, who was one of the president's strongest supporters, was scared and begging for help. President Trump turned him down. So, he tried to call the president's children. Republican House member Mike Gallagher also implored the president to call off the attack."

[multimedia]
Mike Gallagher: "Mr. President, you have got to stop this. You are the only person who can call this off. Call it off. The election is over. Call it off."

Adam Kinzinger: "President elect Joe Biden also went live on TV to demand that President Trump tell the mob to leave."

[multimedia]
Joe Biden: "I call on President Trump to go on national television now, to fulfill his oath and defend the Constitution, and demand an end to this siege."

Adam Kinzinger: "There was a desperate scramble for everyone to get President Trump to do anything. All of this occurred and the president still did not act. I yield to my friend from Virginia."

Elaine Luria: "Thank you, Mr. Kinzinger. President Trump finally relented to the pleas from his staff, his family, and from Capitol Hill for him to do something more at 4:17, 187 minutes More than three hours after he stopped speaking at the Ellipse. After he stopped speaking to a mob that he had sent armed to the Capitol.

"That's when he tweeted a video telling the rioters to go home while also telling him — them that they were special and that he loved them. By that time although the violence was far from over law enforcement had started to turn the tide, reinforcements were on the way, and elected officials were in secure locations.

"The writing was already on the wall. The rioters would not succeed. Here's what was showing on Fox News, the channel the President was watching all afternoon."

[multimedia]
Unknown: "Dr. Brett Baer with more information now. Brett, what do you have?"

Brett Baer: "You know our Pentagon team, Jen Griffin Lucas Tomlinson, now confirming the Defense Department has now mobilized the entire DC National Guard, 1,800 troops, take several hours as I was mentioning before, to get them up and running. The Army secretary, Ryan McCarthy, is setting up a headquarters at the FBI. You just heard from David Spunt that the FBI is also sending troops to the Capitol."

Elaine Luria: "It's no coincidence then that President Trump finally gave in and went out to the Rose Garden at 4:03. His staff prepared a script for him to read, but he refused to use it. As you can see on the screen, you can see the script is stamped, President has seen. The script said, quote, "I'm asking you to leave the Capitol region now and go home in a peaceful way". The President was urged to stick to the script, but he spoke off the cuff.

"Eric Herscmann and Nick Luna went with the President to film the message in the Rose Garden. Let's hear what they had to say and see the never before seen raw footage of the President recording this video message."

[multimedia]

Unknown: "Ultimately, these remarks that we're looking at here and Exhibit 25 were not the remarks that the President delivered in the Rose Garden. Do you know why the President decided not to use these?"

Nicholas Luna: "I don't know, sir. No, I do not know why."

Unknown: "Did the President use any written remarks to your knowledge or did he just go off the cuff?"

Nicholas Luna: "To my knowledge, it was off the cuff, sir."

Unknown: "[off-mic] When you're ready, sir."

Donald Trump: "You tell me when."

Unknown: "When you're ready, sir."

Donald Trump: "Who's behind me?"

Unknown: "He's gone. He's gone. We're all clear now."

Donald Trump: "I know your pain, I know you're hurt. We had a election — let me say. I know your pain. I know you're hurt. We had an election that was stolen from us. It was a landslide election and everyone knows it, especially the other side, but you have to go home now. We have to have peace. We have to have law and order.

"We have to respect our great people in law and order. We don't want anybody hurt. It's a very tough period of time. There's never been a time like this where such a thing happened where they could take it away from all of us, from me, from you, from our country. This was a fraudulent election, but we can't play into the hands of these people.

"We have to have peace. So go home. We love you. You're very special. You've seen what happens. You see the way others are treated that are so bad and so evil. I know how you feel, but go home and go home in peace."

Jared Kushner: "When I got there, basically the President just had finished filming the video and I think he was basically retiring for the day."

Unknown: "Was there any discussion about the President releasing a second video that day?"

Eric Herscmann: "Not that I recall. When — when he finished his video, I think everyone was like day's over. People are pretty drained."

Unknown: "Were pretty what?"

Eric Herscmann: "Drained."

Unknown: "When we say day — day over are we — there were still people in the Capitol at that point weren't there?"

Eric Herscmann: "There were people in the Capitol. But I believe by this stage law enforcement — I'd have to go back and look, but I believe law enforcement was either there moving in or going to take charge. And I just think people were emotionally drained by the time that videotape was done."

Elaine Luria: "Emotionally drained at the White House? Here's what was happening at the same time at the Capitol. We warn the audience that this clip also contains strong language and violence."

[multimedia]
Unknown: "Keep pushing. Don't lose the momentum. [off-mic] We've got another officer unconscious at the terrace. West Terrace. Everybody, we need [inaudible]. We need strong, angry patriots to help our boys. They don't want to leave. [off-mic]"

Elaine Luria: "While President Trump refused to even lift another finger to help, other leaders honored their oath and acted to clear the Capitol and resume the joint session. For instance, here are never before seen photos and video of Congressional leaders in action during the attack. The video is a portion of a call they had at approximately 4:45 with Acting Secretary of Defense, Chris Miller."

[multimedia]

Mitch McConnell: "We're not going to let these people keep us from finishing our business. So we need you to get the building cleared. Give us the okay, so we can go back in session and finish up the people's business as soon as possible."

Christopher Miller: "Amen, sir."

Chuck Schumer: "Mr. Secretary, it's Senator Schumer, some people here in the Capitol police believe it would us take several days to secure the building. Do you agree with that analysis?"

Christopher Miller: "I'm not on the ground, but I do not agree with that analysis."

Chuck Schumer: "So what is the earliest that we could safely resume our proceedings in the Senate and House chambers? The earliest we could safely resume?"

Christopher Miller: "I — here's my assessment, but I prefer to be on the ground, which I personally would prefer to be right now, but I need to be here. I would say best case, we're looking at four to five hours."

Elaine Luria: "The Vice President also worked the phones from his own secure evacuation location, including conversations with Acting Secretary of Defense Miller and other military leaders. While past President Trump's 4:17 video, let's look at some never before seen photographs of the Vice President during this critical time and hear about the Vice President's conversation with military leaders to secure the Capitol and ensure everyone was safe."

[multimedia]

Mark Milley: "Vice President Pence? There were two or three calls with Vice President Pence. He was very animated and he issued very explicit, very direct, unambiguous orders. There was no question about that. And he was — and I can give you the exact quotes I guess from some of our record somewhere, but he was very animated, very direct, very firm.

"And to Secretary Miller, get the military down here, get the guard down here, put down this situation, etc."

Elaine Luria: "As you heard earlier in the hearing, the President did not call the Vice President or anyone in the military, federal law enforcement, or DC government, not a single person. But General Milley did hear from Mark Meadows. The contrast between that call and his calls with Vice President Pence tell you everything you need to know about President Trump's dereliction of duty.

"Let's listen."

[multimedia]

Mark Milley: "He said this from memory. He said, we have — we have to kill the narrative that the Vice President is making all the decisions. We need to establish the narrative that, you know, that the President is still in charge and that things are steady or stable. Or words to that effect. I immediately interpret that as politics, politics, politics.

"Red flag for me personally, no action, but I remember it distinctly and — and I don't do political narratives."

Elaine Luria: "So while President Trump and his advisors were drained, other leaders upheld their oaths to do the right thing. Maybe it was exhausting to get the President to put out that video, but think about the law enforcement officers who were attacked by the mob that day. And President Trump had summoned them himself to Washington.

"And what about President Trump? He watched TV, tweeted, called Senators to try to delay the count of electoral votes, called Rudy Giuliani, and argued with his staff who were insinuating — who were insisting that he should call off the attack. Ms. Mathews, what was your reaction to President Trump's message to the mob at 4:17?"

Sarah Matthews: "I was struck by the fact that he chose to begin the video by pushing the lie that there was a stolen election. And as the video went on, I felt a small sense of relief because he finally told these people to go home. But that was immediately followed up by him saying, we love you, you're very special. And that was disturbing to me because he didn't distinguish between those that peacefully attended his speech earlier that day and those that we watched cause violence at the Capitol.

"Instead, he told the people who we had just watched storm our nation's Capitol with the intent on overthrowing our democracy, violently attack police officers, and chant heinous, things like, hang Mike Pence, we love you, you're very special. And as a spokesperson for him, I knew that I would be asked to defend that.

"And to me, his refusal to act and call off the mob that day and his refusal to condemn the violence was indefensible. And so I knew that I would be resigning that evening. And so I finished out the work day, went home, and called my loved ones to tell them of my decision and resigned that evening."

Elaine Luria: "Thank you. Indefensible. Let's hear what some of your colleagues in the press office told us about their reaction to the same 4:17 message."

[multimedia]

Judd Deere: "I felt like it was the absolute bare minimum of what could have been said at that point for something on camera."

Unknown: "What else do you think should have been said?"

Judd Deere: "So — a more forceful — a more forceful dismissal of the violence, a more forceful command to go home, a more forceful respect for law enforcement, even a comparison to the respect that we have given law enforcement as it relates to what was done to them in the prior summer. And I thought it was important that an acknowledgment be given to the US Capitol building itself.

"What it's a symbol of, what it means, not only to the people that work there, but to the American people generally, and the work of Congress that by law needed to be conducted that day."

Unknown: "Do you wish in hindsight that the President had asked the protesters to leave the Capitol earlier than he ended up asking them to do that?"

Kayleigh McEnany: "Of course, I would have loved if the go home message would have happened earlier in the day."

Elaine Luria: "The President's words matter. We know that many of the rioters were listening to President Trump. We heard from one last week, Stephen Ayres. Let's listen to what he had to say about the 4:17 message from the President and see how rioters reacted to the President's message in real time."

[multimedia]

Stephen Ayers: "Well, when we were there, as soon as that come out, everybody started talking about it. And that's — it seemed like it started to disperse. You know some of the crowd —"

Unknown: "I'm here delivering the President's message. Donald Trump has asked everybody to go home. [off-mic] That's our order. [off-mic] He says, go home. He says, go home. [off-mic] Yeah. He said to go home."

Elaine Luria: "But just as Mr. Ayres said, police were still fending off the last throes of the brutal assault. I yield to the gentleman from Illinois."

Adam Kinzinger: "While everyone else was working to get Congress back in session, what did President Trump do? At 6:01, just one minute after the citywide curfew went into effect, he posted his last tweet of the day. After officers engaged in multiple hours of hand-to-hand combat with over 100 of them sustaining injuries, President Trump tweeted at 6:01 and justified the violence as a natural response to the election."

Adam Kinzinger: "He said, quote, "these are the things and events that happen when a sacred landslide victory is so unceremoniously, viciously stripped away from great patriots who have been badly, unfairly treated for so long. Go home with love and peace. Remember this day forever. He called the mob great patriots. He told people to remember the day forever. He showed absolutely no remorse. A few minutes later at 6:27 the President left the dining room and he went up to the White House residence for the night.

"On the screen is the last photograph of the President that night as he went into the residence. As he was gathering his things in the dining room to leave, President Trump reflected on the day's events with a White House employee. This was the same employee who had met President Trump in the Oval Office after he returned from the ellipse.

"President Trump said nothing to the employee about the attack. He said only quote, "Mike Pence let me down." Ms. Matthews, what was your reaction to President Trump's 6:01 tweet?"

Sarah Matthews: "At that point, I had already made the decision to resign. And this tweet just further cemented my decision. I thought that January 6th, 2021 was one of the darkest days in our nation's history and President Trump was treating it as a celebratory occasion with that tweet. And so it just further cemented my decision to resign."

Adam Kinzinger: "Others agreed with your assessment of that tweet. Let's look at what they had to say."

[multimedia]
Unknown: **"Who asked you about this tweet before it was sent?"**

Nicholas Luna: **"The President."**

Unknown: **"Tell us about that conversation and everything that you said and he said to the best of your recollection."**

Nicholas Luna: "Sure. So he said what do you think of this. And I believe I saw the text message — or the — on his phone. And I — I remember saying to him the wording on the first sentence — I guess it's one long sentence. But the wording on the first sentence would lead some to believe that potentially he had something to do with the events that happened at the Capitol."

Unknown: "What did he say?"

Nicholas Luna: "I don't recall him saying anything in response to that. And I believe that was the end of the conversation."

Unknown: "Did he change anything in light of your comments?"

Nicholas Luna: "No, Sir, he did not."

Unknown: "And what about this made you think that someone might perceive the President having a role in the violence at the Capitol?"

Nicholas Luna: "It — it was my interpretation of the words. I mean, I'm — I'm not a — you know, I don't write speeches or anything, but the phrase these are the things that happen to me sounded as if — as if culpability was associated with it. To me."

Tim Murtaugh: "I don't think it's a patriotic act to attack the Capitol. But I have no idea how to characterize the people other than they trespassed, destroyed property, and assaulted the US Capitol. I think calling them patriots is, let's say, a stretch to say the least."

Unknown: "Is that all it is, a stretch? Or just flatly wrong?"

Tim Murtaugh: "I don't think it's a patriotic act to attack the US Capitol."

Unknown: "Would you call it unpatriotic?"

Tim Murtaugh: "Criminal. Unpatriotic, sure."

Pat Cipollone: "What happened at the Capitol cannot be justified in any form or fashion. It was wrong and it was tragic and a lot — and it — and it was a terrible day. It was a terrible day for this country."

Greg Jacob: "I thought it was inappropriate."

Unknown: "Why."

Greg Jacob: "To my mind, it was a day that should be remembered in infamy. That wasn't the tenor of this tweet."

Adam Kinzinger: "Despite the violence of the day, the effort to delay the certification continued. That evening, Rudy Giuliani called several of President Trump's closest political allies in the hour before the joint session resumed. Representative Jim Jordan and Senators Marsha Blackburn, Tommy Tuberville, Bill Haggerty, Lindsey Graham, Josh Hawley, and Ted Cruz.

"We know why Mr. Giuliani was calling them, because at 7:02 he left a voicemail for Senator Tuberville which later became public. Let's listen to just the start of it."

[multimedia]

Rudy Giuliani: "Hello. Senator Tuberville? Or I should say Coach Tuberville. This is Rudy Giuliani, President's lawyer. I'm calling you because I want to discuss with you how they're trying to rush this hearing and how we need you, our Republican friends, to try to just slow it down so we can get these legislatures to get more information to you."

Adam Kinzinger: "Mr. Giuliani did not even mention the attack on the Capitol. Instead he was pushing on behalf of President Trump to get members of Congress to further delay the certification. Even though some members did proceed with objections, Vice President Pence and Congress stood firm and successfully concluded the joint session in the early morning hours of January 7th. Here are some of what members of the President's party said in the days and weeks after the attack."

[multimedia]

Mitch McConnell: "There's no question, none, that President Trump is practically and morally responsible for provoking the events of the day. No question about it. The people who stormed this building believed they were acting on the wishes and instructions of their President. And having that belief was a foreseeable consequence of the growing crescendo of false statements, conspiracy theories, and reckless hyperbole which the defeated President kept shouting into the largest megaphone on planet Earth."

Kevin McCarthy: "The violence, destruction, and chaos we saw earlier was unacceptable, undemocratic, and un-American. It was the saddest day I've ever had as serving as a member of this institution."

Chip Roy: "Madam Speaker, today the People's House was attacked which is an attack on the Republic itself. There is no excuse for it. A woman died, and people need to go to jail. And the President should never have spun up certain Americans to believe something that simply cannot be."

Adam Kinzinger: "Well after three in the morning Congress certified the 2020 election results. Soon after, this statement by President Trump was posted on Dan Scavino's Twitter account because the President's account by now had been suspended. As you can see, President Trump stuck with his big lie that the election was stolen, but he did say there would be an orderly transition.

"We learned though that the statement was not necessarily his idea. Jason Miller, a campaign advisor, told us that after the joint session started, he heard nothing from President Trump or the White House about assuring the nation that the transfer of power would take place. So Mr. Miller took it upon himself to draft the statement and call the President at 9:23 that night to convince him to put it out.

"Let's listen to what he had to say about the call."

[multimedia]
Unknown: "Did he disagree with something that you had put in the statement? Some particular word or phrase that — that he did not want included?"

Jason Miller: "I'd say just a — that he wanted to say peaceful transition. And I said that ships kind of already sailed. So we're going to say orderly transition. That was — that was about the extent of disagreement or — or pushback from the conversation."

Adam Kinzinger: "The last person President Trump spoke to by phone that night was Johnny McEntee, his head of personnel. Mr. McEntee told us that they talked about the events of the day and the multiple resignation by — by Administration officials. The decision whether to resign was one that weighed heavily on people in the Administration.

"On the one hand, people like Mr. Pottinger and Miss Matthews here, as proud as they were to have served refused to be associated with President Trump's dereliction of duty. But others were sincerely worried that leaving President Trump to his own devices would put the country at continued risk. Listen to what we heard about that tension from Pat Cipollone, from General Mark Milley, and Eugene Scalia, who was the Secretary of Labor."

> [multimedia]
> **Pat Cipollone**: "And then after that some people were resigning, obviously, over January 6th. We know who they — they were. Did I consider it? Yes. Did I do it? No. Concerned about is if people in the counsel's office left, who would — who would replace me? And I had some concerns that it might be somebody who, you know, had been giving bad advice."

> **Eugene Scalia**: "On the morning of the 7th the decision I arrived at was that the most constructive thing I could think of was to seek a meeting of the cabinet. You know, I thought that trying to work within the Administration to steady the ship was likely to have, you know, greater value than simply resigning, after which point I would have been powerless to really affect things with the Administration."

Pat Cipollone: "Eugene thought that there should be a cabinet meeting."

Unknown: "Do you know why Mark thought it would not be productive?"

Pat Cipollone: "I — I — I don't remember why. I — I think it probably had something to do with Mark's view of how the President might react and that he — you know, but things like that."

Mark Milley: "There was a couple of the calls where, you know, Meadows and or Pompeo, but more Meadows, you know, how — how is the President doing? Like, Pompeo might say how's the President doing? And Meadows would say, well, he's in a really dark place. Like here's one, for example, on the 7th of January. So this is a day after, right?

"POTUS is very emotional and in a bad place. Meadows."

Adam Kinzinger: "As you heard Secretary Scalia wanted President Trump to convene a cabinet meeting. He put his request in a memo to the President and here's what it said. You can see that Secretary Scalia recommended that the President quote, "No longer publicly question the election results after Wednesday, no one can deny this is harmful." Secretary Scalia also highlighted the importance of the public knowing the President would invoke his cabinet in decision making and not quote "certain private individuals." Though Secretary Scalia did not say it, he was referring to Rudy Giuliani and the rest of the so-called clown car working with President Trump to try to overturn the election.

"Secretary Scalia understood that the President needed to do more to reassure the public about the last few weeks of the Trump Administration. Mr. Pottinger, when you made the decision to resign, did — did you walk out of the White House immediately?"

<u>Matthew Pottinger</u>: "No, I wanted to first talk to my immediate boss. That was the National Security Advisor Robert O'Brien. Robert O'Brien was traveling on the 6th. I reached him at about 4:30 p.m. and told him that I was submitting my resignation. He accepted the resignation. But he also asked whether I could stay until he could get back to the White House.

"And — and I agreed to that. We — we both wanted to make sure that I was leaving in a responsible way. We — we still have foreign adversaries to worry about, you know, hackers, terrorists, nation states. And I did not want to leave my chair empty given that I was the top national security staffer in the White House.

"So I ended up staying at my desk through the night. When Robert O'Brien arrived back at the White House the next morning, the morning of the 7th, I debriefed with him and left for the last time."

<u>Adam Kinzinger</u>: "So you and I both share a passion for national security of our country. Can you share with me what's your view on how January 6th impacted our national security?"

<u>Matthew Pottinger</u>: "Well, when — when you have a Presidential transition, even under the best circumstances it is a — it's a time of vulnerability. It's a time of vulnerability for, you know, when you have a contested election — I was certainly concerned that some of our adversaries would be tempted to probe or test US resolve.

As an example, in late December the Iranian government attacked the US embassy in Baghdad. They did that using some of their terrorist proxies. President Trump did handle that. He — he sent a very clear warning to the Ayatollah and his regime, which I think had a - - had a useful effect. I — I think that we would have handled other threats of that nature, and luckily no other threats materialized before the inauguration on the 20th. But our national security was harmed in a different way by the 6th of January.

"And that is that it — I — I think it emboldened our — our enemies by helping give them ammunition to feed a narrative that our system of government doesn't work, that the United States is in decline. China, the — the Putin regime in Russia, Tehran, they're fond of pushing those kinds of narratives. And by the way, they're wrong.

"The — you know, we've been hearing, for the entirety of US history from kings and despots, that the United States is — is in decline, and those kings and despots have been proven wrong every single time. But nonetheless, January 6th helped feed a perception that I think emboldens our adversaries. You know, the — the other part I — I think is simply our — our allies.

"I heard from a lot of friends in Europe, in Asia, allies, close friends, and supporters of the United States that they were concerned about the health of our democracy. And so, I think it's incumbent upon us to put their minds at ease, to put our own hearts at ease, by investigating what happened on the 6th and making sure that it never happens again."

Adam Kinzinger: "Look, I've always said democracies are not defined by bad days. They're defined by how they recover from those bad days. And that's what we're doing here, is to bring accountability to that so we can actually come back even stronger than when we went into January 6th. Ms. Matthews, as you left the White House for the last time that night on January 6th, what did you think Americans needed to hear from President Trump?"

Sarah Matthews: "I think that the American people needed to hear and see him publicly commit to a peaceful or at least orderly transition of power. In the aftermath of the Capitol attack, it wasn't just enough for us to ask him to condemn the violence. He needed to agree that he would peacefully transfer power over to the incoming administration, because that's one of our fundamentals and what it means to live in a democracy.

"And so, that evening when I resigned, the resignation statement that I drafted, I referenced this and I said our nation needs a peaceful transfer of power, in hopes that it would put some sort of public pressure on the White House and President Trump to publicly agree to an orderly transition."

Adam Kinzinger: "Thank you. I yield to my friend from Virginia."

Elaine Luria: "Thank you, Mr. Kinzinger. The staff who remained at the White House on the morning of January 7th knew the president needed to address the nation again. And they had a speech prepared for him that morning, but he refused for hours to give it. As you heard Cassidy Hutchison testify previously, President Trump finally agreed to record an address to the nation later that evening, the evening of January 7th, because of concerns he might be removed from power under the 25th Amendment or by impeachment.

"We know these threats were real. Sean Hannity said so himself in a text message that day to Press Secretary Kayleigh McEnany. He wrote "No more stolen election talk. Yes, impeachment and 25th Amendment are real." We obtained the never before seen raw footage of the president recording his address to the nation that day on

January 7th, more than 24 hours after the last time he had addressed the nation from the Rose Garden.

"Let's take a look."

> **[multimedia]**
> **Unknown**: **"Whenever you're ready, sir."**
>
> **Donald Trump**: **"I would like to begin by addressing the heinous attack yesterday. And to those who broke the law, you will pay. You do not represent our movement. You do not represent our country. And if you broke the law — I can't say that. I'm not gonna — I already said you will pay. The demonstrators who infiltrated the Capitol have defied the seat of — it's defiled, right?**
>
> **"See, I can't see it very well. I'll do this. I'm going to do this. Let's go. But this election is now over. Congress has certified the results. I don't want to say the election's over. I just want to say Congress has certified the results without saying the election's over, okay?"**
>
> **Ivanka Trump**: **"But Congress has — now Congress has—"**
>
> **Donald Trump**: **"Yeah, right."**
>
> **Ivanka Trump**: **"Now Congress."**
>
> **Donald Trump**: **"I didn't say over. So, let — let me see. Don't go to the paragraph before. Okay? I would like to begin by addressing the heinous attack yesterday. Yesterday is a hard word for me."**

Ivanka Trump:" Just take it out. Say heinous attack."

Unknown: "Say heinous attack on our nation."

Donald Trump: "Ah, good. Take the word yesterday out, because it doesn't work with the heinous attack on our country. Say on our country. Want to say that?"

Ivanka Trump: "No, keep it."

Donald Trump: "My only goal was to ensure the integrity of the vote. My only goal was to ensure the integrity of the vote."

Elaine Luria: "On January 7th, one day after he incited an insurrection based on a lie, President Trump still could not say that the election was over. Mr. Pottinger, you've taken the oath multiple times in the Marines and as an official in the executive branch. Can you please share with us your view about the oath of office and how that translates into accepting election results and a transfer of power?"

Matthew Pottinger: "Sure. You know, this isn't the first time that we've had a close election in this country. And President Trump certainly had every right to challenge in court the results of these various elections. But once you've had due process under the law, you have to conform with the law no matter how bitter the result.

"Once you've presented your evidence in court, judges have heard that evidence, judges have ruled, if you continue to contest an election, you're not just contesting an election anymore, you're actually challenging the Constitution itself. You are challenging the societal norms that allow us to remain unified.

"I think that one example, for example, you've got Vice President Richard Nixon back in 1960 had lost a hard fought election against Senator John F Kennedy. There were irregularities in that vote, according to a lot of the histories. And a lot of Vice President Nixon's supporters asked him to fight, contest it, don't concede.

"But in one of his finest moments, Vice President Nixon said no. He said it would tear the country to pieces. And he conceded to Jack Kennedy and announced that he was going to support him as the next president. We have an example of a Democratic candidate for President, Vice President Al Gore, who faced a very similar dilemma.

"He strongly disagreed with the Supreme Court decision that lost his election bid and allowed President George W Bush to take office. But he gave a speech of concession in late December, mid or late December of — of 2000, where he said this is for the sake of the unity of — of us as a people and for the strength of our democracy.

"I also am going to concede. I'm going to have to support the — the new president. His speech is actually a pretty good model, I think, for any candidate of — for any office up to and including the president, and from any party to read, particularly right now. You know, the oath that our presidents take, it's very similar to the oath of office I took as a US Marine officer and the — the oath I took as a White House official.

"It is to — to support and defend the Constitution. It's to protect the Constitution, to bear true faith and allegiance to the Constitution. And it is a sacred oath. It's an oath that we take before our families. We take that oath before God. And I think that we have an obligation to live by — by that oath.

"And I do still believe that we have the most ingenious system of government on earth despite its imperfections. I don't envy countries that don't have this system that actually allows for a predictable, peaceful transfer of government every four to eight years. And it's not something that we should take for granted."

Elaine Luria: "Thank you. As we heard at the start of the hearing, in the immediate aftermath of January 6th, Republican leader Kevin McCarthy understood that President Trump bore responsibility for that day and should have taken immediate action to stop the violence. He was even more candid in calls with Republican colleagues.

"As you'll hear in a moment, recordings of some of these calls that were made were later published by The New York Times. The context for these calls was that a resolution had been introduced in the House calling for Vice President Pence and the Cabinet to remove President Trump from power under the 25th Amendment.

"Let's listen."

> [multimedia]
> **Kevin McCarthy: "I've had it with this guy. What he did is unacceptable. Nobody can defend that and nobody should defend it. The only discussions I would have with him is that I think this will pass and it would be my recommendation he should resign. I mean, that would be my take, but I don't think he would take it, but I don't know.**
>
> **"But let me be very clear to all of you, and I've been very clear to the president. He bears responsibility for his words and actions, no ifs, ands, or buts. I asked him personally today does he hold responsibility for what happened? Does he feel bad about what happened? He told me he does have some responsibility for**

what happened and he needed to acknowledge that."

<u>**Elaine Luria**</u>: "President Trump has never publicly acknowledged his responsibility for the attack. The only time he apparently did so was in that private call with Kevin McCarthy. There's something else President Trump has never acknowledged, the names and the memories of the officers who died following the attack on the Capitol.

"We're honored to be joined tonight by police and first responders who bravely protected us on January 6th. Your character and courage give us hope that democracy can and should prevail even in the face of a violent insurrection. We on this dais can never thank you enough for what you did to protect our democracy.

"On January 9th, two of President Trump's top campaign officials texted each other about the president's glaring silence on the tragic death of Capitol Police Officer Brian Sicknick, who succumbed to his injuries the night of January 7th. His campaign officials were Tim Murtaugh, Trump's director of communications, and one of his deputies, Matthew Wolking.

"Their job was to convince people to vote for President Trump, so they knew his heart, his mind, and his voice as well as anyone, and they knew how he connects with his supporters. Here's what they had to say about their boss. Murtaugh said, "Also shitty not to have acknowledged the death of the Capitol Police officer." Wolking responded, "That's enraging to me. Everything he said about supporting law enforcement was a lie," to which Murtaugh replied, "You know what this is of course?

"If he acknowledged the dead cop, he'd be implicitly faulting the mob. And he won't do that because they're his people. And it would also be close to acknowledging that what he lit at the rally got out of control. No way he acknowledges something that could ultimately be called his fault. No way." President Trump did not then and does not now have the character or courage to say to the American people what his own people know to be true.

"He is responsible for the attack on the Capitol on January 6th. Thank you, and I yield to the gentleman from Illinois."

Adam Kinzinger: "Thank you, Ms. Luria. Tonight's testimony and evidence is as sobering as it is straightforward. Within minutes of stepping off the Ellipse stage, Donald Trump knew about the violent attack on the Capitol. From the comfort of his dining room, he watched on TV as the attack escalated. He sent tweets that inflamed and expressed support for the desire of some to literally kill Vice President Mike Pence.

"For three hours, he refused to call off the attack. Donald Trump refused to take the urgent advice he received that day, not from his political opponents or from the liberal media, but from his own family, his own friends, his own staff, and his own advisers. In the midst of an attack when there was no time for politics, the people closest to Trump told him the truth."

Adam Kinzinger: "It was his supporters attacking the Capitol and he alone could get through to them, so they pled for him to act, to place his country above himself. Still, he refused to lead and to meet the moment to honor his oath. It was only once the vice president and the members of Congress were in secure locations and the officers defending the Capitol began to turn the tide that then President Trump engaged in the political theater of telling the mob to go home. And even then he told them all they were special and that he loved them. Whatever your politics, whatever you think about the outcome of the election, we as Americans must all agree on this. Donald Trump's conduct on January 6th was a supreme violation of his oath of office and a complete dereliction of his duty to our nation.

"It is a stain on our history. It is a dishonor to all those who have sacrificed and died in service of our democracy. When we present our full findings, we will recommend changes to laws and policies to guard against another January 6th. The reason that's imperative is that the forces Donald Trump ignited that day have not gone away.

"The militant intolerant ideologies, the militias, the alienation and the disaffection, the weird fantasies and disinformation, they're all still out there ready to go. That's the elephant in the room. But if January 6th has reminded us of anything, I pray it is reminded us of this, laws are just words on paper.

"They mean nothing without public servants dedicated to the rule of law and who are held accountable by a public that believes oath matters — oaths matter more than party tribalism or the cheap thrill of scoring political points. We — the people must demand more of our politicians and ourselves. Oaths matter.

"Character matters. Truth matters. If we do not renew our faith and commitment to these principles, this great experiment of ours, our shining beacon on a hill, will not endure. I yield to the gentlewoman from Virginia."

Elaine Luria: "Thank you, Mr. Kinzinger. Throughout our hearings, we've provided many facts and painted a vivid picture of the events of January 6th. The violence, the human toll, both emotional and physical, including the tragic loss of life, the threats to our Constitution, the rule of law, and the danger to this nation, a nation we all love as Americans.

"In tonight's hearing, we've gone into great detail about the events inside the White House on January 6th. We've described how the President of the United States who was bound by oath to the Constitution and by duty to ensure the laws are faithfully executed, took no action when the cornerstone of our democracy, a peaceful transition of power, was under attack.

"But it's more than that, Donald Trump summoned a violent mob and promised to lead that mob to the Capitol to compel those he thought would cave to that kind of pressure. And when he was thwarted in his effort to lead the armed uprising, he instigated the attackers to target the Vice President with violence, a man who just wanted to do his constitutional duty.

"So in the end, this is not as it may appear, a story of inaction in a time of crisis, but instead it was the final action of Donald Trump's own plan to assert the will of the American people and remain in power. Not until it was clear that his effort to violently disrupt or delay the counting of the election results had failed did he send his message — a message to his supporters in which he commensurated with their pain and he told them affectionately to go home.

"That was not the message of condemnation and just punishment for those who broke the law that we expect from a President whose oath and duty is to ensure the laws are faithfully executed. But instead, It was his newest version of Stand Back and Stand By. To me, this is personal. I first swore an oath to support and defend the Constitution against enemies, foreign and domestic, when I entered the US Naval Academy at age 17. I spent two decades on ships at sea defending our nation from known and identifiable foreign enemies who sought to do us harm.

"I never imagined that that enemy would come from within. I was not as pression [ph] as Abraham Lincoln who 23 years before the Civil War said, if destruction be our lot, we must ourselves be its author and its finisher. Donald Trump was the author. And we the people, for ourselves and our posterity, should not let Donald Trump be the finisher.

"Thank you. And I yield to the Vice Chair."

Liz Cheney: "Thank you very much, Mrs. Luria. I want to thank our witnesses for joining us today. The members of the Select Committee may have additional questions for today's witnesses and we ask that you respond expeditiously in writing to those questions. Without objection, members will be permitted ten business days to submit statements for the record, including opening remarks and additional questions from our witnesses.

"I'd now like to turn things to Chairman Thompson for a few closing words."

Bennie Thompson: "The members of the committee and I appreciate and thank all persons who have come forward voluntarily to provide information to help protect our democracy, and our work continues. As we've made clear throughout these hearings, our investigation is going forward. We continue to receive new information every day.

"We are pursuing many additional witnesses for testimony. We will reconvene in September to continue laying out our findings to the American people and pushing for accountability. In the first hearing of this series, I asked American people to consider the facts and judge for themselves. The facts are clear and unambiguous.

"I thank the American people for their attention over the past several weeks. I wish you all a pleasant evening."

Liz Cheney: "And let me again thank our witnesses today. We've seen bravery and honor in these hearings. And Ms.

Matthews and Mr. Pottinger, both of you will be remembered for that. As will Cassidy Hutchinson. She sat here alone took the oath and testified before millions of Americans. She knew all along that she would be attacked by President Trump and by the 50, 60, and 70 year old men who hide themselves behind executive privilege.

"But like our witnesses today, she has courage and she did it anyway. Cassidy, Sara, and our other witnesses including Officer Caroline Edwards, Shaye Moss and her mother, Ruby Freeman, are an inspiration to American women and to American girls. We owe a debt to all of those who have and will appear here.

"And that brings me to another point. This committee has shown you the testimony of dozens of Republican witnesses, those who served President Trump loyally for years. The case against Donald Trump in these hearings is not made by witnesses who were his political enemies, it is instead a series of confessions by Donald Trump's own appointees, his own friends, his own campaign officials, people who worked for him for years, and his own family.

"They have come forward and they have told the American people the truth. And for those of you who seemed to think the evidence would be different if Republican Leader McCarthy had not withdrawn his nominees from this committee, let me ask you this, do you really think Bill Barr is such a delicate flower that he would wilt under cross- examination?

"Pat Cipollone, Eric Herscmann, Jeff Rosen, Richard Donoghue? Of course they aren't. None of our witnesses are. At one point in 2016 when he was first running for office Donald Trump said this, I could stand in the middle of Fifth Avenue and shoot somebody and I wouldn't lose any voters. That quote came to mind last week when audio from Trump advisor, Steve Bannon, surfaced from October 31st, 2020, just a few days before the Presidential election.

"Let's listen."

[multimedia]
Steve Bannon: "And what Trump's going to do is declare victory, right? He's going to declare victory, but that doesn't mean he's a winner. He's just gonna say he's a winner. The Democrats — more of our people vote early that count. Theirs vote in mail. And so they're going to have a natural disadvantage and Trump's going to take advantage — that's our strategy.

"He's gonna declare himself a winner. So when you wake up Wednesday morning, it's going to be a firestorm. Also — also if Trump is — if Trump is losing by 10 or 11:00 at night, it's going to be even crazier. Because he's gonna sit right there and say they stole it. If Biden's wining, Trump is going to do some crazy shit."

Liz Cheney: "And of course, four days later, President Trump declared victory when his own campaign advisors told him he had absolutely no basis to do so. What the new Steve Bannon audio demonstrates is that Donald Trump's plan to falsely claim victory in 2020 no matter what the facts actually were was premeditated. Perhaps worse, Donald Trump believed he could convince his voters to buy it whether he had any actual evidence of fraud or not.

"And this same thing continued to occur from Election Day onward until January 6th. Donald Trump was confident that he could convince his supporters the election was stolen no matter how many lawsuits he lost, and he lost scores of them. He was told over and over again in immense detail that the election was not stolen.

"There was no evidence of widespread fraud. It didn't matter. Donald Trump was confident he could persuade his supporters to believe whatever he said no matter how outlandish and ultimately that they could be summoned to Washington to help him remain President for another term. As we showed you last week, even President Trump's legal team led by Rudy Giuliani knew they had no actual evidence to demonstrate the election was stolen.

"Again, it didn't matter. Here's the worst part. Donald Trump knows that millions of Americans who supported him would stand up and defend our nation were it threatened. They would put their lives and their freedom at stake to protect her. And he is preying on their patriotism. He is preying on their sense of justice.

"And on January 6th, Donald Trump turned their love of country into a weapon against our Capitol and our Constitution. He has purposely created the false impression that America is threatened by a foreign force controlling voting machines or that a wave of tens of millions of false ballots were secretly injected into our election system or that ballot workers have secret thumb drives and are stealing elections with them.

"All complete nonsense. We must remember that we cannot abandon the truth and remain a free nation. In late November of 2020, while President Trump was still pursuing lawsuits, many of us were urging him to put any genuine evidence of fraud forward in the courts and to accept the outcome of those cases. As January 6th approached, I circulated a memo to my Republican colleagues explaining why our Congressional proceedings to count electoral votes could not be used to change the outcome of the election.

"But what I did not know at the time was that President Trump's own advisors, also Republicans, also conservatives, including his White House counsel, his

Justice Department, his campaign officials, they were all telling him almost exactly the same thing I was telling my colleagues. There was no evidence of fraud or irregularities sufficient to change the election outcome.

"Our courts had ruled it was over. Now we know that it didn't matter what any of us said because Donald Trump wasn't looking for the right answer legally or the right answer factually. He was looking for a way to remain in office. Let's put that aside for a moment and focus just on what we saw today. In our hearing tonight, you saw an American President faced with a stark and unmistakable choice between right and wrong.

"There was no ambiguity. No nuance. Donald Trump made a purposeful choice to violate his oath of office, to ignore the ongoing violence against law enforcement, to threaten our constitutional order. There is no way to excuse that behavior. It was indefensible. And every American must consider this, can a President who is willing to make the choices Donald Trump made during the violence of January 6th ever be trusted with any position of authority in our great nation again?

"In this room in 1918, the Committee on Women's Suffrage convened to discuss and debate whether women should be granted the right to vote. This room is full of history and we on this committee know we have a solemn obligation not to idly squander what so many Americans have fought and died for. Ronald Reagan's great ally, Margaret Thatcher, said this, let it never be said that the dedication of those who love freedom is less than the determination of those who would destroy it. Let me assure every one of you this, our committee understands the gravity of this moment, the consequences for our nation.

"We have much work yet to do and we will see you all in September. I request those in the hearing room remain seated until the Capitol Police have escorted witnesses and members from the room. Without objection, the committee stands adjourned."

Made in the USA
Columbia, SC
16 March 2023

13899119R00048